ROCK 'N' ROLL

THE ROCK 'N' ROLL YEARS

Wise Publications
London/New York/Sydney/Cologne

Exclusive distributors:
Music Sales Limited
8/9 Frith Street, London W1V 5TZ, England.

Music Sales Pty Limited
120 Rothschild Avenue, Rosebery, NSW 2018, Australia.

This book © Copyright 1989 by
Wise Publications
UK ISBN 0.7119.1672.1
Order No. AM72646

Art direction & design by Mike Bell
Compiled by Peter Evans
Typeset by Capital Setters

Music Sales' complete catalogue lists thousands of
titles and is free from your local music shop, or direct from
Music Sales Limited. Please send £1 in stamps for postage to
Music Sales Limited, 8/9 Frith Street, London W1V 5TZ.

Printed in the United Kingdom by
Courier International Limited, Tiptree, Essex.

Summertime Blues

Words & Music by Eddie Cochran & Jerry Capehart

Save The Last Dance For Me

Words & Music by Doc Pomus & Mort Shuman

gon-na be ___ So dar-lin', ___ save the last dance for

me. Oh, I me. Ba-by, don't you know I

love you so? ___ Can't you feel it when we touch?

I will nev-er nev-er let you go. ___ I love you, oh, so

much. You can dance, go and car-ry on ___ till the

night is gone ___ and it's time to go. ___ If he

asks if you're all a-lone, ___ can he take you home, ___ you must

tell him no. ___ 'Cause don't for-get who's tak-ing you home and in whose arms you're

gon-na be. ___ So, dar-lin', ___ save the last dance for

me.   You can   me. _____

9

Sea Of Heartbreak

Words & Music by Hal David & Paul Hampton

11

Oh, what I'd give ____ to sail back to shore ____ Back to your arms once ____ more _____ Oh, _____ come to my res - cue _____ Come here to ____ me _____ Take _____ me and keep me _____

Oh Boy

★

Words & Music by Sunny West,
Bill Tilghman & Norman Petty

All of my love, all of my kiss-in', You're gon-na see what

you been miss-in', OH, BOY!__ When you're with me, OH, BOY!__ The

world can see that you were meant for me.____ All of my life

ev-ry-thing right, I'm gon-na have some fun to-night!_ All o' my love,

all o' my kiss-in', You're gon-na see what you been miss-in', OH, BOY!_

When you're with me, OH, BOY!_ The world can see that you were

meant for me._____ me._____

Puppy Love

Words & Music by Paul Anka

Gm7   C7   F

love _____ just be - cause we're in our teens,

Am7   Dm7   Gm7   C7

Tell them all it is - n't fair _____ to take a - way my on - ly

F   Gbmaj7   F   F7   Bb

dream. _____ I cry each night my

Bbm   F   C7   F   F7   Bb

tears _ for you, my tears are all ___ in vain. _____ I'll hope ___ and I'll pray ___ that ___

may - be some-day you'll be back in my arms once a - gain. Some-one help me, help me

please,_____ is the an - swer up a - bove?

How can I, how can I tell them___ This is not a pup - py

love._____ And they called it pup-py love._____

C'mon Everybody

Words & Music by Eddie Cochran & Jerry Capehart

1. Well, C'M - ON, EV - 'RY - BOD - Y, And let's get to - geth - er to - night!
2. (Well, my) ba - by's num - ber one, But I'm gon - na dance with three or four,
3. (Well, we'll) real - ly have a part - y, But we got - ta put a car out - side,

I got some mon - ey in my jeans And I'm
And the house - 'll be shak - in' From my
If the folks come home I'm a -

real - ly gon - na spend it right! Been a -
bare __ feet __ slap-pin' the floor. _____ When you
fraid they gon - na have my hide. _____ There'll be

F   G7   F

do - in' my home work all week long, Now the house is emp - ty, the
hear __ that mus - ic your feet won't sit still. If your broth - er won't, __ then your
no __ more mov-ies for a week or two; No more run-nin' a - round __ with the

G7   (Shout)   C

folks   are   gone. { Oo,   oo!' }
sis - ter will.   { Oo,   oo!' }   C'M - ON, EV - 'RY-BOD - Y!
us - u - al crew.   { Who   cares. }

F   G7   C

F   G7 | 1. 2. C | | 3. C

                                      2. Well, my
                                      3. Well, we'll

21

Jailhouse Rock

Words & Music by Jerry Leiber & Mike Stoller

EXTRA CHORUSES

4. The sad sack was a-sittin' on a block of stone,
    Way over in the corner weeping all alone.
    The warden said, "Hey buddy, don't you be no square,
    If you can't find a partner, use a wooden chair!"
    Let's rock, etc.

5. Shifty Henry said to Bugs, "For Heaven's sake,
    No one s lookin', now's our chance to make a break."
    Bugsy turned to Shifty and he said, "Nix, nix,
    I wanna stick around a while and get my kicks,"
    Let's rock, etc.

Blue Suede Shoes

Words & Music by Carl Lee Perkins

Not Fade Away

Words & Music by Charles Hardin & Norman Petty

Bony Moronie

Words & Music by Larry Williams

She's a real up - set - ter she's real live wire Ev-'ry-

bod-y looks when she goes ___ by she's_ a real good

good girl real-ly grabs your eyes. ___ I love her, ___ she loves me ___

Oh, how hap-py now we can be. ___ Mak-ing love un-der-neath the

ap-ple tree. ___ I got a girl, I got a girl. ___

30

To Know You Is To Love You

Words & Music by Phil Spector

To know, know, know, {him}/{you} is to

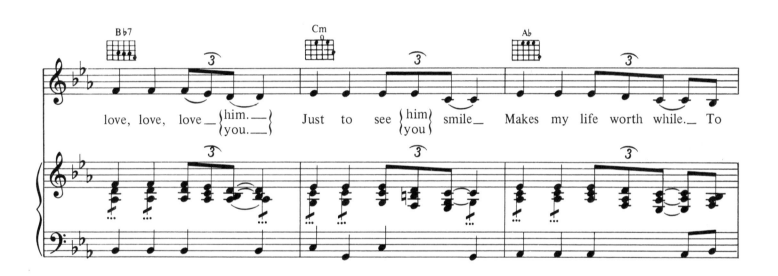

love, love, love {him.}/{you.} Just to see {him}/{you} smile Makes my life worth while. To

know, know, know {him}/{you} Is to love, love, love, {him;}/{you;} And I do

That'll Be The Day

Words & Music by Norman Petty, Buddy Holly & Jerry Allison

you say, good-bye, Yes,__ that-'ll be the day, when you make me cry, Ah, you say you're gon-na leave, you

know it's a lie,_'cause that-'ll be the day____ when I die._ Well, __ when I die.__

When Cu-pid shot his dart, He shot it at your heart, So if we ev-er part and I leave you,

You say you told me 'an you told me bold-ly, That some day, well, I'll be through. Well,

To Verse 2

To Chorus

D.%. al Fine

mf

35

Peggy Sue

★

Words & Music by Jerry Allison,
Norman Petty & Buddy Holly

PEG - GY SUE, ___   PEG - GY SUE, ___

Pret - ty, pret - ty, pret - ty, pret - ty, PEG - GY SUE, ___ Oh, my Peg - gy, ___

My PEG - GY SUE; _____   Oh, well, I

love you gal, ___ and I need you, PEG - GY SUE. ___

I love you,— PEG-GY SUE,— With a love so

rare and true,— Oh, Peg - gy, ——— My PEG - GY SUE; ———

Oh, well, I love you, gal, _ Yes, I want you, PEG - GY SUE.—

Fine

D. S. al Fine

38

Treat Me Nice

Words & Music by Jerry Leiber & Mike Stoller

I know that you've been told It's not fair to tease so if you come on cold, I'm real-ly gon-na freeze. If you don't want me to be cold as ice, Treat me nice.

Make me feel at home If you real-ly care. Scratch my back and

Party Doll

Words & Music by James Bowen & Buddy Knox

Moderato, with a beat

Verse

1. All I__ want is a PAR-TY DOLL,__ To come a-long with me, when I'm feel-in' wild;__ To
2. I saw a gal walk-in' down the street,__ The kind__ of a gal I would love to meet;__ She

be ev-er lov-in' and true and fair,__ To run__ her__ fin-gers a-through my hair.
had blonde__ hair and__ eyes of blue,__ __ Ba-by, I'm a-gon-na have a par-ty with you.

(Tacet)

Refrain

Come a-long and be my PAR-TY DOLL, Come a-long and be my PAR-TY DOLL,

43

Rockin' Robin

Words & Music by Jimmie Thomas

Bright rock tempo

VERSE

1-3 He rocks in the tree-top, all the day long, Hop-pin' and a-bop-pin'and a-sing-in' his song.
2 Ev-'ry lit-tle swal-low, ev-'ry chick-a-dee, Ev-'ry lit-tle bird in the tall oak tree. The

All the lit-tle birds on Jay-bird street, love to hear the rob- in go "Tweet, tweet, tweet!"
wise old owl, the big black crow, flap their wings, sing-in' "Go bird, go."

CHORUS

ROCK-IN' RO - BIN,— ROCK-IN' RO - BIN,—

Blow, ROCK-IN' RO-BIN, 'cause we're real-ly gon-na rock to-night.—

A pret-ty lit-tle ra-ven at the bird band-stand, (patter)

taught him how to do the bop and it was grand. They start-ed go-in' stead-y, and bless my soul, He

out-bopped the buz-zard and the o-ri-ole. He

CODA

Problems

Words & Music by Felice & Boudleaux Bryant

Prob-lems, prob-lems pile up-on my head. _____ Woe is me, I

should have stayed in bed _____ I can't get the car, my marks ain't been so

good. _____ My love life just ain't swing-in' like it should. _____

CHORUS

Prob - lems, prob - lems, prob - lems. They're

all on ac - count of my lov-in' you like I do.

Prob - lems, prob - lems, prob - lems They

won't be solved un - til I'm sure of you. _____ You can solve my prob-lems

with a love that's true. _____ true.

Poor Jenny

Words & Music by Boudleaux & Felice Bryant

ev - 'ry-bod - y scat - tered out for plac-es un-known___ I could-n't car-ry Jen-ny so I

left her a - lone___ Poor Jen-ny___ Well, Jen-ny had her pic-ture in the

pa - per this-a morn - ing, she made it with a bang Ac-

cord-ing to the sto - ry in the pa-per this-a morn - ing, Jen-ny was the lead - er of a

teen-age gang___ Well, Jen-ny has a broth-er and he's hot on my trail___ Her

fath-er wants to ride me out of town on a rail___ I hope I'm still a-round when Jen-ny

gets out of jail.___ Poor Jen-ny.___ 2. I Jen-ny.___

2. I went down town to see her, she was locked in a cell
   She wasn't very glad to see me, that I could tell
   In fact, to tell the truth, she wasn't looking too well
   Poor Jenny
   Her eye was black, her face was red, her hair was a fright
   She looked as though she'd been a-cryin' half of the night
   I told her I was sorry, she said, "Get out of sight"
   Poor Jenny
   It seems a shame that Jenny had to go get apprehended
   A heck of a fate
   This party was the first one she had ever attended
   It had to happen on our very first date
   Well, Jenny has a brother and he's hot on my trail
   Her father wants to ride me out of town on a rail
   I hope I'm still around when Jenny gets out of jail
   Poor Jenny.

Itsy Bitsy, Teenie Weenie, Yellow Polkadot Bikini

Words & Music by Lee Pockriss & Paul J. Vance

Why Do Fools Fall In Love

Words & Music by Frankie Lymon & Morris Levy

Oo - wah, oo - wah,___ oo - wah, ___ oo - wah,_

oo - wah, ___ oo - wah,_ why___ do fools ___ fall in love?_

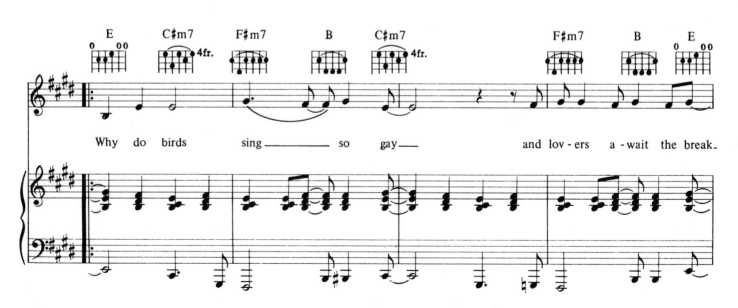

Why do birds sing _____ so gay___ and lov - ers a - wait the break._

Tell me why.

Why do

fools fall in love?

Repeat and fade

Mony Mony

Words & Music by Bobby Bloom, Ritchie Cordell,
Bo Gentry & Tommy James

Wake Up Little Susie

Words & Music by Felice & Boudleaux Bryant

61

we'd be in by ten.   Well,   Su - sie ba - by, looks

like we goofed a - gain _____   Wake Up _____ Lit - tle   Sus - ie _____

Wake Up _____ Lit - tle Sus - ie _____   We've got - ta go

home.

D.S. al Coda
w/repeat

CODA

Bird Dog

★

Words & Music by Boudleaux Bryant

64

VERSE 2. Johnny sings a love song *(Like a bird)*
He sings the sweetest love song *(You ever heard)*
But when he sings to my gal *(What a howl)*
To me he's just a wolf dog *(On the prowl)*
Johnny wants to fly away and puppy love my baby *(He's a bird dog)*
(CHORUS)

3. Johnny kissed the teacher *(He's a bird)*
He tiptoed up to reach her *(He's a bird)*
Well, he's the teacher's pet now *(He's a dog)*
What he wants he can get now *(What a dog)*
He even made the teacher let him sit next to my baby. *(He's a bird dog)*
(CHORUS)

Rock Around The Clock

Words & Music by Max C. Freedman & Jimmy de Knight

One, two, three o'-clock, four o'-clock rock,

five, six, sev-en o'-clock, eight o'-clock rock, Nine, ten, e-lev-en o'-clock,

twelve o'-clock rock, We're gon-na rock a-round the clock to-night.___

F

1. Put your glad rags on and join me, Hon,__ We'll__ have some fun when the
(2. When the) clock strikes two, and three and four,__ If the band slows down we'll__
(3. When the) chimes ring five and six and seven,__ We'll be rock - in' up in __
(4. When it's) eight, nine, ten, e - lev - en, too,__ I'll be go - in' strong and__
(5. When the) clock strikes twelve, we'll cool off, then, Start a - rock - in' 'round the__

F7   Bb9

clock strikes one,__ We're gon - na rock a - round the clock to - night, We're gon - na
yell for more,__ We're gon - na rock a - round the clock to - night, We're gon - na
sev - enth heav'n,__ We're gon - na rock a - round the clock to - night, We're gon - na
so will you,__ We're gon - na rock a - round the clock to - night, We're gon - na
clock a - gain,__ We're gon - na rock a - round the clock to - night, We're gon - na

F   G7   Gm7 C7+5 C9sus 1 F

rock, rock, rock, 'til broad day - light, We're gon - na rock, gon - na rock a - round__ the clock__ to - night.__

2 F

2. When the
3. When the
4. When it's
5. When the

All I Have To Do Is Dream

Moderately

Words & Music by Boudleaux Bryant

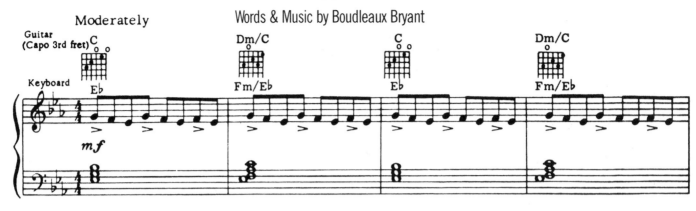

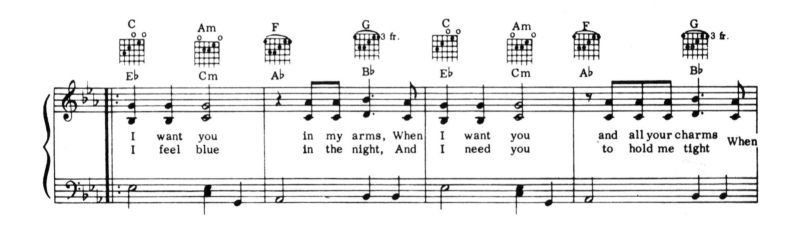

Raining In My Heart

Words & Music by Boudleaux & Felice Bryant

Bye Bye Love

Words & Music by Felice & Boudleaux Bryant

There goes my ba - by___ with some - one new;___ She sure looks
(I'm through with) ro - mance,___ I'm through with love;___ I'm through with

hap - py;___ I sure am blue.___ She was my
count - ing___ the stars a - bove.___ And here's the

ba - by___ till he stepped in;___ Good- bye to
rea - son___ that I'm so free:___ My lov - in'

Sad Movies (Make Me Cry)

Words & Music by John D. Loudermilk

I saw my dar-ling and my best friend walk in ___

Though I was sit-ting there, they did-n't see ___ And

so they sat right down in front of me ___ And when he kissed her

lips, I al-most died ___ And in the mid-dle of the col-or car-

True Love Ways

Words & Music by Buddy Holly & Norman Petty

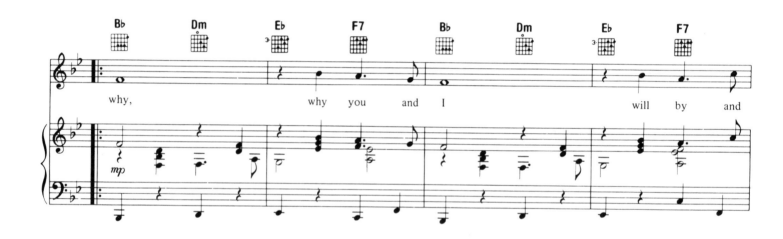

Put Your Head On My Shoulder

Words & Music by Paul Anka

Put your head on my should - er, Hold me in your arms, Ba - by.

Squeeze me oh so tight, Show me that you love me too. ____

____ Put your lips close to mine, dear. Won't you kiss me once, Ba - by?

Oh, Pretty Woman

Words & Music by Roy Orbison & Bill Dees

Oh,_____ Pret - ty   Wom - an

Oh,_____ Pret - ty   Wom - an

I Fought The Law

Words & Music by Sonny Curtis

I fought the law and the law won
I fought the law and the law won I

left my ba-by and I feel so bad I guess my race is run She's the best girl

I've ev-er had I fought the law and the law won I fought the law and the

law won

A

Chantilly Lace

Words & Music by J.P. Richardson

Only You (And You Alone)

Words & Music by Buck Ram & Ande Rand

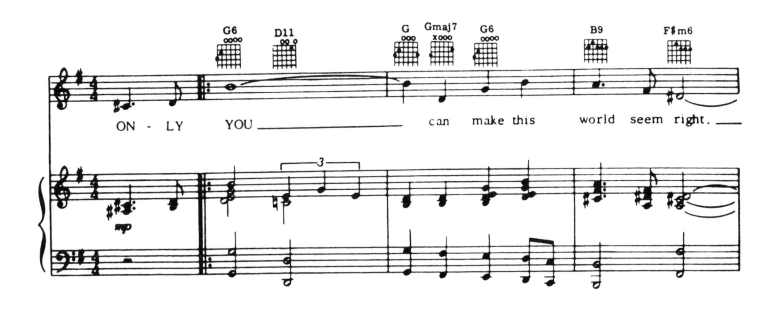

ON - LY YOU _____ can make this world seem right. ___

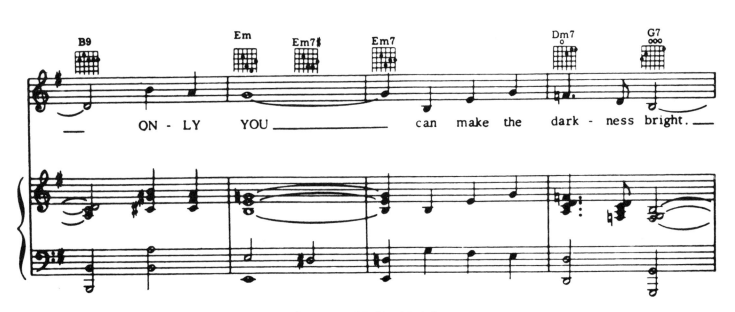

— ON - LY YOU _____ can make the dark - ness bright. ___

Lucille

Words & Music by Richard Penniman & Albert Collins

Lu - cille, Won't you do your sis - ter's will?
cille, Please come back where you be - long.
cille, Ba - by, sat - is - fy my heart.

Oh, Lu - cille, Won't you do your sis - ter's will?
Oh, Lu - cille, Please come back where you be - long.
Oh, Lu - cille, Ba - by sat - is - fy my heart.